Frequently Asked Questions About

Smoky Mountain Black Bears

by Courtney Lix

Great Smoky Mountains Association

Printed in the United States of America by Lithographics, Inc.

4   5   6   7   8   9   10

ISBN 978-0-937207-61-1

Edited by Steve Kemp and Kent Cave

Designed by Karen Key

Editorial Assistance by Julie Brown and Valerie Polk

Great Smoky Mountains Association is a private, nonprofit organization which
supports the educational, scientific, and historical programs of Great Smoky
Mountains National Park. Our publications are an educational service intended
to enhance the public's understanding and enjoyment of the national park. If you
would like to know more about our publications, memberships, guided hikes and
other projects, please contact:

Great Smoky Mountains Association

P.O. Box 130

Gatlinburg, Tennessee 37738

(865) 436-7318

www.SmokiesInformation.org

Photography Credits

Bill Lea: Front and back cover, 3, 4, 7, 9, 10, 11, 12, 13, 14, 16, 17, 18-19, 21, 22
(black cherries, squawroot, spring beauties, and mountain ash), 23, 24, 26-27, 28,
30, 31, 32, 34, 35, 36, 37, 41, 42, 43, 44, 51, 55, 56, 57, 60-61

Mary Ann Kressig: 45

Howie Garber: 8

Great Smoky Mountains National Park Archives: 38, 39, 46, 47, 48, 49

Michael J. Gadomski: 22 (yellow jacket)

Ann Froschauer: 22 (salamander), 52, 53

Acknowledgments

Thank you to Dr. Frank Van Mannen of the University of Tennessee and Dr. Mike Vaughan at Virginia Tech for answering my questions and explaining the particulars of bear survival and mortality statistics to me, and to Bill Lea for sharing his observations from countless hours spent watching and photographing black bears.

To Annette Hartigan for providing me with a myriad of bear information from the park's library, and Steve Kemp for impeccable editing, as always.

And more thanks to National Park Service wildlife biologists Kim Delozier and Bill Stiver who also took time out of their very busy schedules working with the Smokies' current bear population to review my manuscript for accuracy and offer comments from their extensive experiences in the national park.

Thank you to Dr. Michael Pelton and his multitude of committed, courageous, and curious students from the University of Tennessee, for decades of groundbreaking work on black bears in the Smokies. Without your findings, this book would not have been possible. (...and how did you ever find so many people willing to climb 60 feet up a tree in the middle of nowhere in the middle of winter to stick their heads in a small den containing a mother bear and her cubs?).

How many species of bears live in the Smokies?

1

The black bear (*Ursus americanus*) is the only bear species found in Great Smoky Mountains National Park, and it is the park's second largest native mammal, smaller only than the elk. Black bears, which inhabit forested areas from Maine to California and Canada to Mexico, have a much wider distribution than the other two bear species found in North America.

Although it's often said that the highest peaks in the Smokies are biologically similar to Canadian landscapes, you still won't find any brown bears here. Brown and polar bear habitats are confined to more northern areas, like Alaska and Canada. The grizzly bear, which is a subspecies of brown bear, also inhabits parts of the northern Rocky Mountains but does not occur in the eastern United States.

What is the bear population in Great Smoky Mountains National Park?

2

Approximately 1,500 bears live in the national park—about two bears per square mile. This is one of the highest density populations in North America, and one reason why the black bear has become a symbol of the Smokies. When the national park was created in 1934, it was estimated there were possibly fewer than 100 black bears left in the Smokies. By the 1970s, the bear population was estimated at 300-500 individuals, boosted by the reduction in hunting pressure and regeneration and maturation of forest habitat, and has increased steadily since.

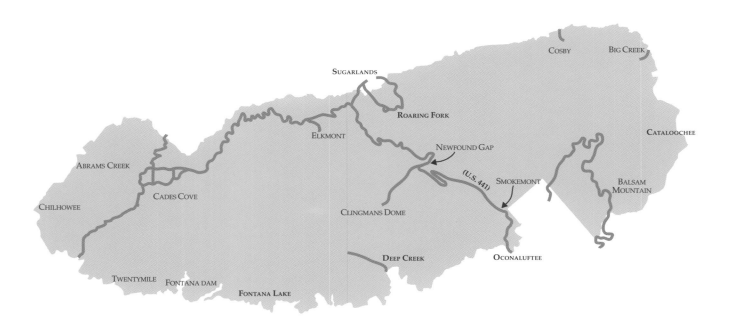

Bears go where the food is: oak trees, berry bushes, cherry trees, and grape vines all attract bears.

What habitats do Smoky Mountain black bears prefer?

3

Black bears live just about anywhere there are a lot of trees, and this makes most of Great Smoky Mountains National Park ideal black bear habitat. They prefer relatively inaccessible (by human standards) areas of oak/hickory forests with thick understory of rhododendron, mountain laurel, and berry bushes, where they can easily hide and forage for food. The Cades Cove area of the park can support a particularly high density of bears because of the many white oak trees, cherry trees, and berry bushes, including blackberry, blueberry and huckleberry. Black bears are highly adaptable, though, and can even live in small isolated habitats near suburban neighborhoods or outskirts of major cities if there is enough food and shelter available.

What are the distinctive physical characteristics of Smoky Mountain black bears?

4

If you happen to get a good look at a Smoky Mountain black bear, you'll probably notice its thick, black fur, prominent slightly-pointed ears, and long, tan-colored muzzle. Black bears also have small, close-set eyes, and their claws are curved as a special adaptation for climbing trees. Many black bears have such shaggy fur that their short tails are almost completely hidden, and they often look clumsy when they walk because their back legs are longer than their front legs, a characteristic that helps them climb trees.

Are all black bears actually black?

5

British Columbia's "spirit bear."

Bears in the Smokies are always black, but in other parts of the world their fur can be brown (called "cinnamon"), and even pale bluish-gray or white (British Columbia's rare "spirit bears"). Bear biologists studying the Smokies' population have found, however, that about fifteen percent of cubs are born with a white patch, called a "blaze," on their chests. A few bears with white paws have also been reported in the Sugarlands area of the park. During the summer, you might see bears in the Smokies with patches of brownish hair, but this will eventually be replaced by a thick, black winter coat.

? 6 What kind of sensory abilities do black bears have?

Smell is one of the most important senses for bears: their noses have more than a hundred times the smell receptors of a human nose. Just as humans often navigate using visual maps, it's believed that bears find their way around based on an "olfactory" or smell map. Bears also have excellent hearing and will often sense a person hiking on a trail and disappear into the forest so quickly that the human will never know the bear was there. Like humans, bears have color vision, but they're nearsighted, so they rely much less on sight than their other senses when looking for food and detecting danger.

How big are black bears?

7

The largest wild bear ever live captured in the national park was a male that weighed 400 pounds, and the largest female weighed 227 pounds. A male bear poached near the park boundary weighed 620 pounds, but it was reported that this bear relied on garbage rather than natural foods so its size was probably due to an unnatural diet. The average summer weight of an adult female bear (called a sow) in the Smokies is between 120-130 pounds, and an adult male generally weighs between 200-240 pounds—during the fall, however, they can gain up to 3-5 pounds daily and nearly double their weight in a season! A bear's weight fluctuates dramatically throughout the year, because in addition to gaining weight in the fall, it may lose a third or more of its body weight during the winter denning season and into the spring, until food becomes readily available.

The average black bear in the Smokies is a bit smaller than bears to the north.

Black bears are the smallest of the North American bear species, and bears in the Smokies are, on average, smaller than black bears found elsewhere in the country. This doesn't mean they're not big animals though: an adult bear is usually three to three and a half feet tall at the shoulder, and can reach over six feet when it stands on its hind legs.

The discrepancy in size of Smokies bears has two causes: first, although it's inside a national park, the black bear habitat here doesn't produce as much food per acre as areas like eastern North Carolina and Pennsylvania. Studies have shown that

although the Smokies have reasonably productive food sources, they are not as productive or consistent from year to year.

The second reason that bears are smaller here than elsewhere is that, because of protection from hunting, the density of bears in the Smokies is higher than in other places and this increased competition for food may result in some bears being excluded from certain productive areas by dominant bears.

When bears were moved from the national park to the Big South Fork National River and Recreation Area (located in north-central Tennessee and southern Kentucky) for an experimental reintroduction, they gained a significant amount of weight, which scientists attribute to the combination of access to very productive food sources and less competition for space with other bears.

With so many bears in the national park, how likely am I to see one?

8

Wild black bears are naturally shy and afraid of humans. They often smell or hear humans long before a person has any idea a bear is nearby, and quickly disappear into the forest. A bear encounter is most likely to happen when a good food source (blackberry bushes or cherry trees, for example) is within sight of a road or trail. While feeding on high quality foods, a bear may be more tolerant, even with people or other bears around. During such an encounter, visitors should keep their distance and never approach the bear. Park regulations state that visitors cannot intentionally approach a bear closer than 50 yards.

During summer and early fall, bears seek out fruits and berries. Black cherries (above) and blackberries (below).

When are bears most active?

9

Bear activity depends a lot on the individual bear and its habitat. Bears are crepuscular (krey-PUS-kyoo-lar) which means they're active in the early morning and at dusk. Bears that live in forests where hunting is allowed, however, may exhibit more nocturnal (active at night) behavior as a response to hunting pressure, especially in areas more commonly frequented by humans.

During the heat of the day, many Smokies bears will rest and stay cool in "day beds," sleeping areas on the ground that are often concealed by thick underbrush. Bear behavior varies with the season and is also highly individualistic, so some bears may naturally be more active in the daytime, especially if they're hungry or during breeding season.

Clockwise from top left: The hind feet of bears share similarities with the feet of humans. Bear scat usually includes obvious clues to a bear's recent diet (black cherries). Bears use their claws to tear apart rotting logs and mark standing trees.

What kinds of sign do bears leave behind?

10

Tracks

Bears walk "plantigrade," which means they keep their heels on the ground, like humans do, which helps them keep their balance when they stand up on their hind legs. They also have five toes on both their front and back paws. Thus, the track of a bear's hind foot looks a lot like a human footprint, just a little wider and shorter, and with five long claw prints!

Scat

The appearance of bear scat varies depending on diet, but it's usually darkly colored because of the bear's largely vegetarian diet, and will often contain indigestible plant matter like seeds, bark, and nut shells. There may also be bits of insect exoskeletons.

Other

Bears may turn over large rocks or tear apart rotting logs, looking for ants, beetles, and other insects. They dig holes in the ground in order to unearth yellow jacket nests and eat the hornets and their larvae. Male bears sometimes stand on their hind legs and claw or bite bark off trees. They probably do this to signal territory possession, but the entire purpose of making these "bear trees" is still not well-understood.

How long do bears live?

11

In general, a bear cub's likelihood of survival through its first year is 87% while it's still being protected by its mother. Mortality rises sharply for young bears (1-3 years old), particularly males, which have about a 57% likelihood of survival. The biggest danger for these yearlings is older bears that may attack and kill them. In addition, other critters like coyotes and bobcats will also attack young bears. There have even been a few instances where a cub was bitten by a rattlesnake and died. If a bear makes it to its fourth birthday, however, it has probably grown large enough not to have to worry about predators any more, and it has probably figured out where to find enough food and shelter. If it's a female, it has a 91% chance of survival, while a male's is slightly lower at 89%.

Bears that lose their fear of humans and become accustomed to eating garbage, however, are more likely to be hit by cars or shot by poachers or legal hunters outside park boundaries. A "beggar" or nuisance bear's life expectancy is much shorter than a wild bear's.

How do biologists determine how old a bear is?

Biologists sedate bears and pull a small, non-functional tooth to determine their age.

While a bear is sedated, researchers extract a small, nonfunctional tooth, usually the first upper or lower pre-molar. Like trees, bear teeth have growth rings, called cementum-annuli, so a biologist can examine a cross-section of the tooth under a microscope and count the number of rings to tell a bear's age.

12

Can bears swim?

13

Yes. Black bears, even when they're cubs, are good swimmers, and have been seen swimming across Fontana Lake. They can easily swim up to a mile and a half.

Are bears fast?

14

Their top speed is thirty miles per hour, but they can only move that quickly over a short distance. To put that pace in perspective, the park's elk, deer, and coyotes can run about forty to forty-five miles per hour, but an average human male's top speed is only fifteen to eighteen miles per hour (world-record holding sprinters can reach twenty-seven miles per hour).

How smart are bears?

15

They're extremely intelligent, although it's not completely understood how smart they are because they're so shy and secretive. Black bears have been called "the other intelligent omnivore" (compared to humans) and some researchers believe bears are second in intelligence only to primates and humans, although a bear brain is only about a third the size of a human brain. A bear was once observed carefully positioning a log across a stream—even using her nose to press the end of the log into the sandy bank to make sure it didn't roll when she stepped on it—so she could cross the water without getting her feet wet. Bears are also notoriously good at figuring out how to get into dumpsters, garbage cans, bird feeders, and cars. Their combination of strength, resourcefulness, and intelligence has given rise to many park legends: for example, many years ago, a bear broke into a Volkswagen and found a feast of fried chicken in a picnic basket in the backseat. Ever afterward, the bear patrolled parking lots and campgrounds, targeting *only* Volkswagens, in the hope of another tasty meal.

Bears can also remember how to get to important wild food sources—a grove of white oaks or a large berry patch—that they went to when they were cubs many years before.

Are bears good at climbing trees?

16

Black bears are tree-climbing experts and can scoot up a tree nearly as fast as a squirrel, despite their bulk. They grasp the tree trunk with the claws on their forepaws, which are curved and adapted for climbing, and push up with their strong hind legs, repeating this procedure in a series of quick, jumping motions until they're high in the branches. When they want to get down, they wrap their legs around the trunk and slide down, rump first. Sometimes they'll jump the final 5-10 feet to the ground.

What do bears eat?

17

Almost anything, from berries and tree bark to salamanders, grass, acorns, cherries, yellow jacket wasps, leaves, trash, and white-tailed deer. Like humans, bears are omnivores, but their diet is about eighty-five percent plant-based, and they're known to eat more than 50 different kinds of plants in the Smokies.

When they emerge from their dens in springtime, there isn't a lot of food available, so they eat grasses, new buds on trees, bark, and squawroot (a fleshy, parasitic plant that grows on tree roots). Insects and insect larvae are a good source of protein, and they'll also eat hornets, chipmunks, yellow jackets, and anything else they can get their paws on.

From top left: black cherries, squawroot, salamander, spring-beauty (bears eat the underground corms), American mountain-ash berries, yellow jacket wasp (the larvae are eaten).

In the summer and early fall, as much as forty percent of a bear's diet consists of berries: blackberries, raspberries, mountain-ash berries, huckleberries, serviceberries, blueberries. Cherries are also an important food source, especially in August. This is known as "soft mast." Then in the fall, when the oak trees begin producing acorns, the bears' diet changes to "hard mast" which includes oak, beech, and hickory nuts. The bears' climbing ability gives them an advantage over deer, wild hogs, and other animals that also eat acorns and hickory nuts because they can climb onto thick branches and feed by ripping the more slender limbs off, devouring the nuts, then sliding farther down the branch to continue feeding, instead of having to wait for the nuts to fall to the ground.

They're good scavengers, too, and will eat carrion (dead animals) and garbage when they find it. But they're also capable of hunting and killing large prey like adult white-tailed deer, especially those that are sick or injured. Opportunistic hunters, they prey upon deer fawns and elk calves, and in the days when people farmed in the Smokies, bears were known to attack calves, pigs, cows, and mules. Before cattle were permanently removed from Cades Cove, farmers reported that bears killed an average of five calves each year.

In late 2008, park fisheries biologists were reintroducing native brook trout to Lynn Camp Prong in the Tremont area of the national park, and part of their work involved removing non-native rainbow trout, which were placed in submerged baskets until they could be relocated. While the biologists were busy at the river, however, some clever black bears discovered the fish baskets and helped themselves to an easy meal!

Bears prefer white oak acorns over other hard mast.

What's the most important food for bears?

18

Acorns, especially white oak acorns, provide the majority of carbohydrates that bears in the Smokies need to put on their layer of fat which helps them survive through the winter and early spring. In September and October, bears may gain up to five pounds a day from eating acorns. They travel long distances to find productive oak groves and other fall foods, moving in what park biologists call the "Fall Shuffle."

Do bears really like honey?

19

Yes, but they also really like to eat the bees and larvae along with the honey—the insects are a good source of protein. The bears' thick fur provides good protection from bee stings, although their noses and faces are still vulnerable. They'll whimper from the stings, and occasionally use their paws to protect their sensitive noses, but they keep on eating.

A bear investigates a hornet's nest, interested in the larvae that may be inside. Bears are one of the reasons that wasps, hornets, and bees defend their nests so aggressively.

Do bears in the Smokies hibernate?

20

Mountaineers used to say that "the bears had gone to house" to describe the winter denning season, which extends from November until April. It's not true hibernation, which is characterized by extreme slowing of an animal's breathing, heart rate, and metabolism—but bears in the Smokies do go into "semi-hibernation" in which they sleep for several months, waking up occasionally on warmer winter days, but they still don't generally eat or drink during this period. Sows with cubs are the first to den, followed by single females and finally, males. The reverse is true for emerging from the dens: the males come out toward the end of March or early April, and females with newborn cubs emerge toward the end of April into May.

Where do bears make their dens?

21

Although the national park has an abundance of hollow logs, rock ledges, and downed trees, the bears here seem to prefer large tree cavities which occur 20 to 60 feet off the ground. These hollow spaces are formed by lightning and decay, and give better protection from human disturbance and rough weather than a den on the ground. A bear will den anywhere it's protected from snow, rain, and cold winds, though, and most dens are only slightly larger than the bear itself, which prevents heat loss during sleep. Some males simply scratch together a pile of leaves and curl up, but pregnant females generally spend a little more time preparing their dens, lining them with ferns or grass for better insulation. Sometimes a bear den will even resemble a giant bird nest on the ground!

Bears den in hollow logs, under boulders and stumps, and in large, standing trees.

? Do bears use the same den year after year?

22

No, they move around to different dens each winter and it's extremely rare that they use the same den twice. They begin selecting a denning site during middle or late November and curl up to sleep soon thereafter.

How do bears know when to seek a den and go into semi-hibernation?

23

The strongest signal is an instinctive awareness to begin looking for a den in the early stages of winter, called an innate "circannual rhythm." Their behavior is also triggered by other cues such as colder temperatures and decreasing availability of food. If a bear hasn't put on enough fat to survive the winter, which can happen in years when the hard mast gets killed by a late frost, the bear will still enter hibernation. If the bear uses up its stored fat supply before spring, it may emerge from its den to try to find food, or, if no food is available, it may stay in the den and metabolize its own tissues (muscles, organs) which would eventually mean starvation.

Do bears have territories?

24

Male bears have large territories—20 to 60 square miles—which are too big to defend completely, but when they encounter an intruder, they'll run them off. During mating season, females establish smaller territories of about two to six square miles which overlap with males' territories. They will defend their space from other females.

Some bears have exhibited remarkable "homing ability" regarding their territories. Bears that have been relocated to other areas, either inside or outside the park, sometimes return to their home ranges within days or weeks. In the late 1980s, Bear #75 became famous for walking over 200 miles to get back to the Smokies (he was removed because of his habit of breaking into the Cable Mill in Cades Cove). Bear #75 was captured and relocated eleven times, resulting in his walking at least 1,500 miles total in his journeys back to Cades Cove.

When do bears mate?

25

Breeding season in the Smokies is in June and July. Males and females are at least three or four years old before they begin breeding. Females generally breed every other year because the cubs stay with their mothers for about eighteen months; males generally breed every year. Male bears may travel long distances looking for mates, sometimes leaving their home territories, but bears are not monogamous, nor do they mate for life.

Cubs learn early in life trees offer food, safety, and a place to scratch your cheeks and back.

When are cubs born?

26

Cubs are born from mid-January to mid-February. Although a female may have mated in July, she still might not have cubs if she didn't find enough food during the fall. Bears reproduce using a mechanism of "delayed implantation," which means that even though a female has mated, a fertilized egg will only become a fetus if the mother has found a sufficient amount of food and stored enough body fat. If she hasn't, she doesn't give birth that year.

Cubs stay with their mothers for about 18 months before striking out on their own.

Are mother bears awake when they give birth?

Since cubs are born during the winter denning period, it's believed mother bears are asleep while they give birth, only waking up to care for the cubs after the birth occurs.

How many cubs are in a litter?

28

The number of cubs born is strongly influenced by the amount of food, specifically acorns, that the sows were able to eat in the fall. After an exceptionally productive acorn year, a sow may give birth to as many as five cubs, but the average litter is two or three cubs.

How much does a cub weigh?

29

At birth, a cub usually weighs half a pound and is the size of a baseball. Cubs are born "altrical," which means "not well developed." They're deaf, blind, toothless, and have almost no hair. They gain weight quickly, though—sow's milk is 30% fat, compared to only 4% in human breast milk—so when they leave the den in late April, cubs weigh between four and seven pounds.

Do black bears live in groups?

30

Males and females without cubs are solitary wanderers. Cubs stay with their mothers through their first year, even sharing a den with her in the winter, but are weaned and must fend for themselves by the summer of the following year, when they're about a year and a half old. This yearling stage is tough for bears because they have to forage for food by themselves but have no established home range. Consequently they're often trespassing on the ranges of larger, older bears and can't rely on their mothers for protection.

Females in the Smokies have been sighted with as many as five cubs.

What's the most difficult time of year for bears in the Smokies?

31

Early spring—March through May—when they've just emerged from their dens. During this time, bears have used up most of the energy in their fat layers, but there's still not a lot of food for them to eat until late June when the berries ripen. For these first few months, bears will often continue to lose weight, and starvation is a constant threat. Records indicate that most black bear attacks on humans occur in May, which is likely related to this stressful, hungry time of year for bears.

What kind of noises do bears make?

Bears don't vocalize often, but they make several distinctive sounds. A sow will make a "woof-woof" noise to warn her cubs of danger and send them scrambling up a tree. When cubs are nursing or warm, they hum happily, but when they're frightened, they bawl like a human baby. It's said that an adult bear in pain can scream in a way that sounds eerily like a terrified woman, and at least one Smokies hunter has sworn off bear-hunting forever after hearing it. Bears also bawl, moan, and bellow when they're confronting other black bears.

People will often hear a bear blow air through its jaws, making an aggressive huffing noise accompanied by the clacking of its teeth. This means the bear is scared, agitated, or feels threatened. While huffing, a bear may also make a short lunge toward whatever has frightened it and stomp its paws on the ground, which means "back off." These are usually bluff charges, and the bear will soon turn tail and run away.

32

How close can I get to a bear and be safe?

33

Bears have individual temperaments, so it's impossible to establish a set distance that's always correct. The official park regulation imposes a fine of up to $5,000 and/or imprisonment of up to six months on anyone who approaches a bear closer than fifty yards (150 feet) or any distance that disturbs the animal. A good rule of thumb is that if the bear (or any other wildlife, for that matter) changes its behavior because of you, you're too close and should retreat slowly. It's much safer to use binoculars, a spotting scope, or a telephoto lens to get a close-up look at a wild animal.

Because bears sometimes look "cute" or resemble humans in certain ways, people occasionally get the wrong idea about them. They are quick, powerful wild animals capable of killing a deer. Approaching a bear is like approaching a 200 pound wild dog that has very sharp claws.

What's a "bear jam"?

34

A bear jam occurs when the traffic backs up, sometimes for miles, usually on Newfound Gap Road or in Cades Cove, because people have stopped their cars in the road to take photos or watch a bear. Please don't be the cause of one. If you spot a bear, use a roadside pullout to do your viewing.

Once a bear has eaten human food or garbage, is it too late for it to return to being a truly wild bear?

35

Not necessarily. The park's wildlife management team responds quickly to reports of nuisance bears, evaluates the behavior of the animal, and then takes appropriate measures. If a bear has only begun to lose its fear of humans, they employ "aversive conditioning" techniques such as catching it in a culvert trap or shooting at it with rubber buckshot (which doesn't hurt the bear, but scares it). This is often enough to frighten a bear away from humans.

Bears conditioned to human food lose their wildness and become pathetic beggars and garbage scavengers.

Basically, the negative experience associated with a place where humans gather (aversive conditioning) must be greater than the positive experience of finding human food or garbage.

If a bear persists in approaching people, it will be caught and relocated at least forty miles from where it encountered humans, which often means it must be removed from the national park. As a last resort, if a bear is judged to be a threat to humans, it must be euthanized.

Have bears attacked people in the national park?

36

With sharp teeth, long claws, and strong legs, even a small black bear is capable of hurting a human, but they're not usually aggressive. In the early days of the national park, the "no feeding" policy was less strictly enforced than it is today, and there were many more bear-human incidents. Many park visitors during the 1940s, '50s, and '60s witnessed scenes of bears emerging from garbage cans along Newfound Gap Road and people proffering food from their picnic baskets to cubs. As a result of this human-bear-food interaction, there was an all-time high of 148 bear "incidents" in 1960, although the most personal injuries (23) were reported

Feeding bears resulted in so many injuries to humans and the relocation of so many bears that the Park Service had to crack down.

Seeing a bear rummage through a garbage can is a very different experience from glimpsing a wild bear roaming through the forest.

in 1966. Alarmed by the increasing conflict between bears and humans, and the bears' loss of their natural fear of humans, the park began conducting research on bear populations and habits and used these new studies to help revise its bear management plan.

Since the late 1960s, park policy has focused on educating visi-

tors about the dangers (both to themselves and the bears) caused by feeding or approaching bears, by giving fines and arrests if necessary, and by controlling the behavior of bears by deterring them from approaching humans. Today, bears rarely attack people in Great Smoky Mountains National Park, preferring to bluff and retreat, but have been known to nip or cuff people who try to feed or pet them, or get too close with a camera. Sows are usually protective of their cubs, but even they prefer to bluff-charge a human in the hope of scaring it away, rather than attack immediately.

Although extremely rare, there have been a couple of significant bear-human incidents in the past decade. In August 2008, an 86-pound male yearling attacked eight-year-old Evan Pala, who was playing in Le Conte Creek near the Rainbow Falls Trail. Evan's father fought the bear off, and it was later shot and taken to the

Educating the public has long been the key to successful bear management in national parks.

University of Tennessee Veterinary School for analysis, but was pronounced to be free of rabies. Indeed, there has never been a recorded instance of a rabid bear in the park. Evan was treated for puncture wounds and scratches, and his father was treated for minor cuts, but they were soon released from the local hospital. The victims were not carrying food, nor did they approach the bear, so it was considered a predatory attack.

In the history of Great Smoky Mountains National Park, only one person has been killed by a bear. Glenda Ann Bradley was a local 51-year-old woman who was hiking by herself near Little River Trail in June 2000 when she was killed by a 113 pound female bear and a yearling cub. Both bears were killed by park rangers.

It is important to remember, however, that even though these incidents receive a lot of media attention, bear attacks in the Smokies are extremely rare—only one or two minor human injuries are caused by bears, on average, each year. If you think a black bear is after your food and it physically attacks you, separate yourself from your food and back away. If you think a black bear is not after your food and it attacks you, fight back like your life depends on it: the bear may consider you to be prey.

How often do rangers have to kill bears?

37

Only one or two bears are euthanized a year, on average. These bears have either displayed unusually aggressive or predatory behavior toward humans or become so food-conditioned that they break into cars or buildings, or rip into tents to get human-related foods.

With so many bears and humans in the national park, what do rangers do to prevent conflicts?

38

The fundamental principle of bear management in the Smokies is keeping human food and garbage away from bears. The park uses bear-proof garbage cans and dumpsters, which require a human's jointed fingers in order to release the latch, and therefore protect the bears from eating picnic scraps instead of wild berries and acorns.

During the summer, picnic areas close at 8:00 p.m. At Cades Cove and the Chimneys picnic areas, which are very popular with visitors, the park maintenance staff works late into the evening to make sure all human food

and garbage is cleaned up before they leave. Rangers enforce food storage regulations by issuing fines to violators, and there are food storage cables near almost every backcountry campsite.

If aggressive bear activity is reported in an area, rangers also close campsites and post signs warning hikers to be alert and cautious.

Wild bears are naturally afraid of humans—cubs mostly learn this fear from their mothers—and if they're not rewarded with food for approaching areas that carry the smell of people, they'll be able to live safer, healthier lives.

The smell of food can cause bears to overcome their natural fear of humans and become dangerous.

Is there a bear hunting season?

Bear hunting is prohibited in the national park. Bear populations are "self-regulating" which means that their population size is determined by the amount of food available, so overpopulation isn't a problem, even without hunting. When the park was established in 1934, because of a combination of logging and overhunting, the bear population was on the verge of collapse, estimated at only 50-200 bears. Hunting is allowed outside the park in both Tennessee and North Carolina, and some bears move into and out of the park as the seasons change, so the population size is constantly changing, but healthy and stable.

What should I do if I'm hiking and I see a bear?

40

If you see a bear, remain watchful. Do not approach it. If your presence causes the bear to change its behavior—that is, if it stops feeding, turns its head to watch you, or changes its travel direction—you're too close. Being too close to a bear may cause it to act aggressively: running toward you, making loud noises, or swatting the ground with its paws. The bear is demanding more space, and you should slowly back away while watching the bear's reaction. Don't run. Try to increase the distance between you and the bear—and the bear will probably do the same.

If a bear persistently follows or approaches you without vocalizing or paw swatting, try changing the direction you're walking. If the bear continues to follow you, stop walking and stand your ground. If the bear gets closer, talk loudly or shout at it. Act aggressively and try to intimidate the bear. If you have companions, gather together as a group to be more intimidating, and make yourselves look as large as possible (move to higher ground, for example, to appear taller). Throw non-food objects  such as rocks at the bear, and use a deterrent like a stout stick if necessary. However tempting it may be, resist the urge to run away—this is dangerous because it requires you to turn your back toward the bear, and increases the likelihood that you'll trip and hurt yourself, making you more vulnerable and sending a signal to the bear that you may be prey.

Also, don't leave food for the bear because this encourages further problems. If the bear's behavior indicates that it's after your food and you're physically attacked, separate yourself from the food and slowly back away. If you run, it may trigger the bear's predatory instincts and it may pursue you instead of being appeased by your food. If the bear shows no interest in your food and you're physically attacked, fight back aggressively.

You should report all bear incidents that occur within the park to a ranger immediately by calling (865) 436-1230. Bear incidents that occur outside the park boundaries should be reported by calling the Tennessee Wildlife Resources Agency at 1-800-332-0900 or the North Carolina Wildlife Resources Commission at (919) 707-0050.

How do hikers and campers keep their food safe from bears?

41

It's very important to keep food put away in a secure place between meals (in a car or suspended from cables), and to keep food out of tents. At night, when camping in the backcountry, nearly all shelters and sites have a cable system to suspend food bags and backpacks. If a bear appears while a person is cooking, it can often be scared back into the woods by clapping, yelling and throwing rocks and sticks.

If you are camping in a campground, or when you're parked at a trailhead for a day hike, you can avoid problems by storing coolers and food containers in the trunk of your car, which keeps it out of sight and reduces the likelihood a bear will see or smell your dinner and help itself to your hamburgers. Some bears have learned to associate food with the sight of a cooler or other food containers and steal or damage those, even though no food is stored in them. Never, ever keep any food in your tent, and clean up immediately after cooking and eating.

A good rule of thumb when you're in bear country is to make sure everything you own smells as little like food as possible: a bear was once caught trying to break into a car, and as best the rangers could figure out, it was after the coconut air freshener.

Backpackers suspend their food and cooking gear from special cables installed at shelters and backcountry campsites.

Why aren't there fences to keep bears out of the hiking shelters?

42

There used to be a problem with people feeding bears at backcountry shelters—people were tempted to lure bears to the shelter area for a photo opportunity, and felt safe hiding behind the chain-link fence with their cameras. Or, if a person began cooking and a bear appeared, the hiker would flee to the safety of the shelter, allowing the bear to get a good meal. This resulted in the dangerous situation of food-conditioned bears in remote, backcountry areas. Once the fencing was removed, hikers began policing themselves and other campers by becoming more diligent about hanging their packs properly on the cables, defending their food, and not feeding the bears—a safer situation for everyone!

What role does the bear play in Cherokee culture?

43

The Eastern Band of the Cherokee called the bear "Yonah" and respected it as a spiritual guide and important source of sustenance. They believed Kuwa'hi Mountain, now called Clingmans Dome, was the sacred home of the great white bear that ruled the spirit world. The bear was the most powerful creature in the forest, and it was said that the power and strength of the bear was transferred to whomever ate its meat. The forepaw flesh was a special delicacy, and the Cherokee often roasted bear meat on sassafras sticks over hickory charcoal.

No part of the animal was wasted: they made necklaces from bear claws and teeth, carved bones into arrowheads, and wound guts into bowstrings. Bear oil was extremely versatile, and was mixed with natural dyes to make paint, rubbed on skin as an insect repellent, and combined with wild cinnamon for perfume. Some researchers hypothesize that the Cherokee created the grassy balds, unusual open spaces found on several Smokies' mountaintops, as game lures for easily ambushing bears.

Necklaces with bear teeth taken from a Cherokee burial mound in 1939.

Were bears important to early European-American settlers in the mountains?

44

Bears were just as important to the European-American mountain folk as they were to the Cherokee. The mountaineers ate bear meat, spun bear fur into thread, made hats, and used bearskin rugs to keep warm. A man named John T. McCaulley caught a bear that had been killing his hogs in Cades Cove, skinned it, and decorated the interior of his 1929 Chevy with bear fur.

Settlers often hunted bears with dogs, and a shrub that grew in thick patches along mountainsides became known as "doghobble" because bears could run through the thickets, but hound dogs would get caught in it and lose the scent of their quarry. "Black Bill" Walker, a settler in the Tremont area of the park, claimed to have killed over 100 bears with his 12.5 pound homemade rifle called "Old Death." Bear hunting, however, was time-consuming and risky, and many families preferred to catch a bear in a "live trap" and put it in a pen, fattening it up through the summer like the rest of their livestock. This is how places like Bearpen Hollow, off Newfound Gap Road, and Bearpen Gap, near Hazel Creek, got their names. In the fall, the settlers would slaughter the fattened bear, providing enough meat to feed the family for a month.

Left: "Black Bill" Walker and his rifle called "Old Death."
Opposite: Mountain families took great pride in their abilities to hunt bears and other wild game. Some bear traps were massive, nearly four feet in length and weighing up to 70 pounds.

Is there a problem with bear poaching in the Smokies?

45

When the national park was established in 1934, local people were accustomed to hunting bears and didn't pay much attention to the federal regulations that protected bears within the new park's boundaries. The poaching problem continued into the late 1980s, prompted by the high prices a bear's gallbladder (an organ that helps the animal digest fat) could bring on the Asian black market—up to $500 dollars for a large gallbladder, which is believed to have medicinal and aphrodisiac properties. Poachers could make over $1,000 from a single bear by also selling the claws for jewelry, the fleshy pads for soup, and hides and heads as trophy items. They would often illegally bait bears with food, or set steel traps in the national park and the surrounding national forests.

In August 1988, "Operation Smoky" became known to the public as the biggest undercover operation focused on poaching in America. State and federal agents spent three years infiltrating the illegal hunting and selling of bear parts, and arrested over 30 people from Tennessee, North Carolina and Georgia. With over half a million acres of bear habitat to protect, it's impossible for rangers to prevent poaching completely, but it appears to have decreased in recent decades.

What are the biggest threats to bears?

In the national park, human garbage and non-native species present the most serious dangers to bears. Losing their fear of humans is dangerous because bears are more likely to exhibit

"panhandling" or "beggar-behavior" along roadsides and be hit by a car, or they may hurt a person and have to be euthanized. These bears are also at greater risk of ingesting food packaging material, like plastic wrappers or chip bags which cause digestive problems, or being shot by a poacher within the national park, or by a legal hunter outside the boundary of the national park.

Wild hogs, a non-native, hybrid species of domestic pig and European wild boar, are another major threat. The hogs compete with bears for food, especially during the critical spring and fall seasons, when food is scarce or the bears are preparing for winter denning. The wild hog is the most prolific large wild mammal in North America. Over an average lifetime, each female hog is capable of producing at least three times the offspring of a female bear, so an uncontrolled hog population would be capable of affecting the Smokies' bear population simply by consuming a significant percentage of the hickory, beech, and oak mast. The hog population in the Smokies is currently estimated to be a few hundred animals and has been brought under control by a vigorous and consistent live-trapping and shooting effort by wildlife field personnel. It is the belief of park wildlife managers that the coyote, which moved into the park in the mid-1980s, preys heavily on the smaller animals (piglets and shoats) and provides a natural control of the pig population.

How do scientists study bears in the national park?

? 47

The partnership between the National Park Service and the University of Tennessee, Knoxville which ran from 1960 to 2008 was the longest continuous study of any bear species that's been conducted in the world. Led by Dr. Michael Pelton, it was one of the first projects to use radio collars in order to learn more about bear movement and habits. Other information was collected by catching a bear in a culvert trap or spring-activated foot snare, then quickly sedating the animal in order to weigh and measure it. Monitoring techniques became more sophisticated through the years, and bears are now lip-tattooed (which is more permanent and less invasive than ear tags), and examined for parasites. A small, non-functional tooth will sometimes be extracted to tell age, and a blood sample will be taken. Sometimes a radio collar is put on the bear so its activity level and location can be monitored, and reproductive history is also tracked for females.

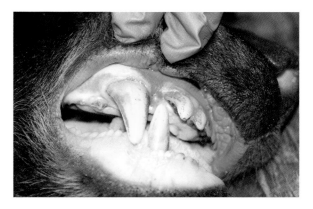

Every July since 1981 the researchers have also conducted the "Bait Station Survey" to estimate distribution and relative density of the bears in the park. Researchers hang open sardine cans from low branches—three cans at a site, at four hundred sites—forming transect lines throughout the park. The tops are peeled open to let the stinky fish smell waft into the forest and attract bears. Although other animals eat the sardines too, there's no mistaking the puncture holes in the sardine cans that were made by bear teeth, or the claw marks on the trees! The percentage of sites visited by bears is converted to a "bear population index" using a numeric formula, which helps park managers monitor population trends.

Researchers have also begun to use DNA analysis to learn about the bear population in a less invasive way. Instead of trapping and sedating the bear to collect information about it, scientists simply surround an area with several strings of barbed wire about a foot and a half off the ground. When the bear squeezes under the wire, lured by open cans of sardines, a bit of its hair gets caught. Only 5-10 hairs are needed in order to determine gender and individual DNA sequence. With this information, scientists can determine population estimates and begin to understand how the bears are related to each other, and their genetic idiosyncrasies. Even though the bears in the Smokies are one of the most well-studied bear populations in the world, there's still much to learn about these intelligent, elusive animals.

Opposite page: A sedated bear is "worked up" near a popular campground.
From top: A "positive" response on a bait station sardine can; bears walk on the heels of their hind feet, like humans; impressive canine teeth and water-soluble ink used for lip tattoo; ear tag used to i.d. individual bears.

Glossary of Terms

Altricial: helpless at birth: blind, toothless, and hairless, and in need of parental care to survive.

Aphrodisiac: a substance that enhances romantic attraction and desire.

Aversive conditioning: bear management technique designed to encourage bears to avoid contact with humans by associating unpleasant experiences (loud noises, confinement in a trap) with the presence, smells and sounds of people. It is only employed when a bear has begun to demonstrate a loss of its natural fear of human beings.

Bait Station Survey: annual summer survey during which sardine cans are placed throughout the park and monitored for bear activity. The number of cans visited by bears compared to the total number of cans set out is used in a mathematical formula to help estimate the bear population in Great Smoky Mountains National Park.

Bear jam: traffic jam, usually on Newfound Gap Road or in Cades Cove, that occurs when people stop to take photos of, or watch a bear but do not move their vehicles to the side of the road so no one can pass and cars sometimes back up for miles.

Bearpen: a wooden enclosure for confining a live bear, usually a yearling, which had been caught by mountaineers. The bear was fed through the summer and fall months and then slaughtered in the late fall.

Beggar bear: a bear that has been fed by humans and consistently approaches them, expecting hand-outs.

Bluff charge: behavior in which a bear stomps its paws on the ground and runs at a person or another bear as if it is going to attack, but shies away at the last moment. Used to indicate that the bear needs more space, or to establish dominance.

Boar: a male bear.

Carrion: the remains of a dead animal.

Cementum-annuli: growth-rings added yearly to a bear's tooth. From these rings, it is possible to tell how old a bear is.

Circannual rhythm: innate biological clock that triggers a certain behavior on a yearly cycle. In black bears, this is the instinct to begin preparing for winter denning.

Crepuscular: active at dawn or early evening.

Culvert trap: a live trap that looks like a sizeable green metal culvert (large pipe often used in drainage under roadways), with a closed end and a hinged door at the other end, and air holes. These traps are often used when wildlife personnel need to catch and relocate a nuisance bear.

Day bed: sleeping area on the ground, often concealed in thick brush, where a bear will rest during the hottest hours of the afternoon.

Delayed implantation: period during which development of a fertilized egg is suspended at an early phase and implantation into the uterine wall is delayed. This is the mechanism by which female bears ensure they don't give birth to more cubs than they can support and enhances cub survival rates.

Euthanize: to administer a lethal dose of anesthetic so that an animal dies painlessly and quickly.

Exoskeleton: hard body covering that protects the soft bodies of some invertebrates, including some insects.

Fall Shuffle: increased bear movement in autumn as bears search out productive stands of nut-bearing trees (oak and hickory) in order to gain weight that will help them survive the winter denning season.

Food-conditioned: a bear that has learned to associate the presence of humans with food. This can result either from being fed directly by people, or from finding garbage or food scraps that have been improperly disposed of.

Gallbladder: an organ that helps an animal digest fat. Asian folklore attributes aphrodisiac properties to bears' gallbladders and they are highly sought-after items on the black market.

Grassy bald: open areas found on the tops of several mountains in the Smokies, inexplicably free of trees; Gregory Bald near Cades Cove and Andrews Bald near Clingmans Dome are the most well-known examples.

Habitat: an area with the particular combination of food, shelter, and space that allows a certain species to establish a population there.

Hard mast: food source characterized by hard shells; for example, acorns, beech and hickory nuts.

Hibernation: the act of spending the winter in a state of deep sleep. Characterized by extreme slowing of bodily processes including breathing, heart rate, temperature, and metabolism.

Indigestible: not able to be converted into energy by an animal's digestive system.

Kuwa'hi Mountain: Eastern Cherokee name for Clingmans Dome, believed to be the dwelling place of the great white bear that ruled the spirit world.

Live trap: a trap that captures an animal without killing or injuring it.

Monogamous: having only one mate in a lifetime or a breeding season.

Mortality: frequency, or likelihood, of death in a population.

Nocturnal: active at night.

Nuisance bear: a bear that has lost its natural fear of humans and either approaches or harasses people for their food, or engages in destructive behavior—breaking into cars, digging through dumpsters, ransacking tents—in its search for human food.

Omnivore: an animal that eats both plants and other animals.

Operation Smoky: the biggest undercover investigation of poaching in American history. The operation made news in August 1988 with the arrest of over thirty people in the Great Smokies region, accused of illegally poaching black bears.

Panhandling: behavior of a food-conditioned bear which approaches people and begs for handouts.

Plantigrade: walking flat on the soles of the feet, like humans do.

Poacher: a person who kills or captures wild animals (or digs up plants) illegally.

Premolars: teeth located behind the sharp cuspids and in front of the large back molars; used to help grind up food.

Regeneration: large scale regrowth or renewal. In the context of the Smokies, this refers to the process by which cleared fields and croplands became forests again after protection as a national park.

Scat: scientific term for animal droppings, also called poop or excrement.

Sedation: a method of calming a wild animal by administering a tranquilizer shot, which temporarily immobilizes it.

Self-regulating population: a population that has biological safeguards built into its reproduction success in order to ensure that the number of individuals in the population does not grossly exceed the available food or space in a given area. In bears, the main safeguard is delayed implantation.

Semi-hibernation: the act of spending the winter in a state of deep sleep, but with less pronounced slowing of bodily processes (breathing, heart rate, temperature, metabolism) than occur during hibernation.

Soft mast: food source characterized by soft, fleshy coverings; mostly fruits and berries, but also dogwood and black gum seeds.

Sow: a female bear.

Squawroot: a small, spiked plant that lacks chlorophyll and resembles an elongated yellow-orange pinecone. It emerges in early spring and is an important food source for bears coming out of winter dormancy.

Territory: a particular area which a bear defends from other bears by confronting and attacking any intruders it encounters.

Transect: an imaginary line through an area along which scientific data is collected. Information collected along transect lines is then used as a representation of the conditions in an entire area.

Yonah: Eastern Cherokee name for the bear, believed to be the most powerful animal in the forest, and respected as a spiritual guide.

Recommended Reading

Becklund, Jack. *Summers with the Bears: Six Seasons in the North Woods.* Hyperion: 2000.

Brody, Allan J. and Michael R. Pelton. 1989. *Effects of Roads on Black Bear Movements in Western North Carolina.* Wildlife Society Bulletin, Vol. 17, No. 1. pp. 5-10.

Chilcoat, Terry S. and Michael R. Pelton. *"A Black Bear Primer."* Country Journal. November, 1975.

Eagle, Thomas C. and Michael R. Pelton. 1983. *Seasonal Nutrition of Black Bears in the Great Smoky Mountains National Park.* International Conf. Bear Res. and Manage. 5:94-101.

Fitzhenry, Dave Taylor. *Black Bears: A Natural History.* Whiteside: 2006.

Herrero, Stephen, Kristy Pelletier, Bernard Peyton, and Christopher Servheen, IUCN/SSC Polar Bear Specialist Group. *Bears: Status Survey and Conservation Action Plan.* Information Press: 1999.

Horstman, Lisa. *The Troublesome Cub.* Great Smoky Mountains Association: 2001.

Linzey, Don and Christy Brecht. *Ursus americanus: Black Bear.* Discover Life in America (www.dlia.org): 2005.

Masterson, Linda. *Living With Bears: A Practical Guide to Bear Country.* PixyJack Press: 2006.

NPS. *Safety in Bear Country.* 2008.

Pelton, Michael. Black Bear. *Wild Mammals of North America.* Eds. JA Chapman and GA Feldhamer. The Johns Hopkins UP. Baltimore and London: 1982. p. 504-514.

Pelton, Michael. *The Black Bear of the Smokies.* TN Conservationist Vol XLIII Nov/Dec 1977 No 8.

Rennicke, Jeff. *Black Bear: Spirit of the Hills.* Great Smoky Mountains Association: 1992.

Rogers, Lynn L. *Watchable Wildlife: The Black Bear.* USDA Forest Service, North Central Forest Experiment Station, St. Paul MI: 1992.

Smith, Howard and Michael H. Francis. *In the Company of Wild Bears: A Celebration of Backcountry Grizzlies and Black Bears.* The Lyons Press: 2006.

Index

About the Author

Courtney Lix was lucky enough to move from Houston, Texas to the Great Smoky Mountains when she was nine. She saw her first wild black bear soon thereafter, while hiking in the Greenbrier area of the national park. She has a degree in ecology and evolutionary biology from Princeton University and is currently an assistant editor at the environmental publisher Island Press, in Washington DC. She returns to the Smokies as often as possible.